FAITH PRAYER & MEDITATION

Spreading Word of God

BISHOP ANGELO H. ROLLE

Dedication

It is with great pleasure by the grace of God, that was given to me to write this book. First and foremost, the dedication of FAITH PRAYER MEDITATION, goes to Almighty God, the King of Kings and the Lord of Lords.

So, then all the glory, all the wisdom for the authorization of this book is the acknowledgement of God's favor upon my life; by faith in Jesus name.

Secondly, acknowledgement dedication goes out to the Body of Christ, for their spiritual support by God's grace, prays fasting and words of encouragement; by faith in Jesus name.

Last but not least, to my wife Marzetta Rolle, my children and siblings; by faith in Jesus' name. Amen.

Acknowledgements

The purpose for the writing of this book, FAITH PRAYER MEDITATION, is to encourage the readers and hearers to empower and to encounter a greater belief and power through, FAITH PRAYER and MEDITATION.

Therefore, through God's Wisdom of FAITH PRAYER and MEDITATION, come the acknowledgement that God have given the readers and hearers the power to transform their lives and the lives of their families, neighbors and every human being on the face of the earth; by faith in Jesus' name. Amen.

Contents

Chapter One

MAGNIFYING GOD

As humans, we have an innate desire to glorify and magnify that which is worthy of praise. Our hearts long to worship and exalt the highest ideals and noblest virtues. In the pages of this chapter, we embark on a journey to explore the beauty and majesty of the divine and to celebrate the splendor of creation itself.

As the psalmist wrote, "Oh, magnify the Lord with me, and let us exalt his name together!" (Psalm 34:3, ESV). Indeed, the glory of God is a theme that runs through the pages of Scripture from beginning to end. From the majestic displays of power in the creation account to the awe-inspiring visions of heaven in the book of Revelation, the Bible portrays a God who is worthy of all honor and adoration.

Through stories, reflections, and meditations, this chapter invites us to join in that chorus of praise and lift our hearts to the One who is worthy of all glory, honor, and power. As we journey together, may our souls be stirred to worship and our spirits be renewed in the presence of the Almighty. As the apostle Paul wrote,

"For from him and through him and to him are all things. To him be glory forever. Amen." (Romans 11:36, ESV).

Let us join in that cry of adoration and praise and magnify the Lord together.

Prayer is a powerful and essential tool in our spiritual journey. It is through prayer that we come before God and lay our hearts and desires before Him. However, the effectiveness of our prayer is not solely based on the words we say or the actions we take but on the condition of our hearts and the alignment of our will with the will of God.

As we are told in Hebrews,

"And without faith it is impossible to please him, for whoever would draw near to God must believe that he exists and that he rewards those who seek him" (Hebrews 11:6, ESV).

Faith is the cornerstone of our relationship with God and our prayer life. When we approach God in faith, we acknowledge His power and sovereignty, and we trust in His goodness and provision.

Furthermore, our prayers must be in alignment with the will of God. Jesus Himself taught us to pray, "Your will be done, on earth as it is in heaven" (Matthew 6:10, ESV). Our desires and requests must be submitted to the will of God, and we must trust that He knows what is best for us.

We must approach God in prayer with our hearts and minds fully focused on Him. It is not enough to simply go through the motions of prayer or recite memorized words. Our prayer must be a reflection of our relationship with God, and we must approach Him with sincerity and authenticity.

In essence, prayer is a powerful tool that requires us to approach God with faith, align our will with His, and fully engage our hearts and minds in His presence. May we all strive to deepen our prayer life and grow closer to God through our petitions and conversations with Him.

The parable of the Pharisee and the tax collector in Luke 18:10-14 teaches us an important lesson about prayer and the acceptance of our requests before God. The Pharisee in the parable prayed with pride and self-righteousness, thanking God that he was not like the tax collector or other sinners. In contrast, the tax collector humbly approached God, acknowledging his sinfulness and asking for mercy.

The crucial difference between the two prayers lies in their alignment with the will of God. The Pharisee prayed according to his own will and desires, focusing on his own accomplishments and righteousness. On the other hand, the tax collector prayed in line with God's will, recognizing his own shortcomings and asking for God's mercy and forgiveness.

This parable teaches us that our prayers must be aligned with the will of God for them to be accepted. When we pray according to our own desires and motivations, we risk missing the mark and falling short of God's plan for our lives. However, when we approach God with humility, seeking His will and guidance, we open ourselves up to the abundance of blessings that He has in store for us.

The will of God must be achieved for our prayers to be accepted because God knows what is best for us. As we align ourselves with His will and trust in His plan for our lives, we can have confidence that our prayers will be heard and answered according to His perfect timing and purpose.

As Christians, prayer is a vital component of our spiritual journey, and it is important that we understand the proper way to approach God in prayer. Jesus Himself taught us how to pray in Matthew 6:9-13 and Luke 11:2-4, instructing us to address God as "Our Father who is in heaven."

"After this manner, therefore, pray ye: Our Father which art in heaven, Hallowed be thy name." Matthew 6:9

And he said unto them, When ye pray, say, Our Father which art in heaven, Hallowed be thy name. Thy kingdom come. Thy will be done, as in heaven, so in earth. Give us day by day our daily bread. And forgive us our sins; for we also forgive every one that is indebted to us. And lead us not into temptation; but deliver us from evil. Luke 11:2-4

By addressing God as our Father, we acknowledge our relationship with Him as children of God and recognize His love, care, and protection over us. We also recognize that God is the ultimate authority and power in the universe and approach Him with reverence and respect.

Furthermore, by directing our prayers to our Father in heaven, we shift our focus away from ourselves and toward God's will and purposes. We acknowledge that God's plans and desires for our lives are greater than our own, and we seek His guidance and wisdom as we navigate the challenges of life.

In addition to petitioning God in prayer, meditation is also an important aspect of our spiritual journey. By meditating on God's Word and His promises to us, we deepen our understanding of His character and develop a closer relationship with Him.

Through prayer and meditation directed to our Father in heaven, we open ourselves up to the transformative power of God's love and grace. As we seek His will and guidance, we can trust that He will lead us on a path of righteousness and fulfill the desires of our hearts according to His perfect plan.

In Luke 18:14, Jesus points out that such vein petitions are characteristic of the unbelievers, who approach God with an attitude of self-importance and worldly wisdom rather than with faith and humility. Jesus emphasizes that the effectiveness of our prayer is not based on our own wisdom or eloquence of speech but on the condition of our hearts and our willingness to surrender to God's will.

In essence, Jesus teaches us that our petitions in prayer must be grounded in humility, faith, and a genuine desire to seek God's will. We must approach God with sincerity and authenticity, acknowledging our own sinfulness and our need for His mercy and forgiveness. By doing so, we open ourselves up to the transformative power of God's love and grace, and our prayers will be heard and answered according to His perfect timing and purpose.

In Matthew 17:21, Jesus says,

"Howbeit this kind goeth not out but by prayer and fasting."

This verse suggests that fasting can be a powerful tool for spiritual growth and overcoming certain obstacles, including spiritual battles.

When approaching a petition through fasting, it's important to first discern the reason for the petition. Is it a personal desire or something that aligns with God's will? It's important to approach fasting with the right heart and intentions.

Fasting involves denying oneself of something, often food, for a set period of time as an act of devotion and surrender to God. The purpose of fasting is to draw closer to God, seek His will and guidance, and develop a deeper intimacy with Him.

When approaching a petition through fasting, the focus should be on seeking God's will and surrendering any personal desires or attachments to the outcome. Fasting can help one to gain clarity and discernment, to focus more on God and less on the petition, and to align oneself with God's purposes.

It's important to note that fasting should not be approached legalistically or as a way to manipulate God into granting one's request. Rather, fasting should be an act of faith and obedience, trusting that God's will is ultimately best and surrendering oneself to His plan.

First, Thessalonians 5:23 says, "May God himself, the God of peace, sanctify you through and through. May your whole spirit, soul, and body be kept blameless at the coming of our Lord Jesus Christ." This verse suggests that God desires for us to be whole and complete, with every aspect of our being surrendered to Him.

Petition involves presenting our requests to God, but it's important to approach this with our entire being, including our spirit, soul, and body. This involves allowing ourselves to be fully present in the moment, with our thoughts and emotions focused on God and His will.

Meditation can be a powerful tool for engaging our entire being in prayer and petition. By quieting our minds and focusing our thoughts on God, we can enter into a deeper level of communion with Him. This allows us to align our desires with His will and to surrender our whole selves to His plan.

When engaging in meditation as part of our petition, it's important to create an environment that supports focus and stillness. This might involve finding a quiet place, eliminating distractions, and using breathing techniques or other methods to calm the mind and body.

As we engage in meditation, we can allow our spiritual and physical selves to manifest, surrendering every aspect of our being to God. This allows us to present our petitions with authenticity and sincerity, trusting that God will hear our requests and respond according to His will.

Meditation has been practiced for thousands of years and is an essential tool for achieving inner peace, clarity of mind, and personal growth. In recent years, scientific research has confirmed the benefits of meditation, showing that it can reduce stress, improve focus, and enhance overall well-being.

For believers, meditation can also be a powerful way to deepen their connection with God and gain spiritual strength. Matthew 22:17-39 contains teachings of Jesus Christ that emphasize the importance of meditation for believers.

In these verses, Jesus is asked which commandment in the Law is the greatest. He responds by saying, "Love the Lord your God with all your heart and with all your soul and with all your mind." (Matthew 22:37). This commandment requires believers to focus their entire being on their relationship with God, which can be achieved through meditation.

Meditation allows believers to quiet their minds and focus their attention on God, which can lead to a deeper understanding of their faith and a stronger connection with God. By meditating regularly, believers can strengthen their faith and become more resilient in the face of life's challenges.

Furthermore, meditation can also help believers develop a greater sense of compassion and love for others, as emphasized in Matthew 22:39, which states, "Love your neighbor as yourself." By cultivating a sense of inner peace and compassion through meditation, believers can extend this love to others and create a more harmonious and peaceful world.

"Only be thou strong and very courageous, that thou mayest observe to do according to all the law, which Moses my servant commanded thee: turn not from it to the right hand or to the left, that thou mayest prosper whithersoever thou goest. This book of the law shall not depart out of thy mouth; but thou shalt meditate therein day and night, that thou mayest observe to do according to all that is written therein: for then thou shalt make thy way prosperous, and then thou shalt have good success." Joshua 1: 7-8

But his delight is in the law of the LORD; and in his law doth he meditate day and night. And he shall be like a tree planted by the rivers of water, that bringeth forth his fruit in his season; his leaf also shall not wither; and whatsoever he doeth shall prosper.
Psalms 1: 2-3

The concept of praying or making petitions in the name of Jesus Christ is a central aspect of Christian belief and practice. It means that believers are approaching God in prayer as if Jesus Himself were making the request. This idea is rooted in the teachings of the Bible, including the passage in Philippians 2:8-11.

In this passage, the apostle Paul writes about the humility and exaltation of Jesus Christ. He explains that Jesus, although He was in the form of God, humbled Himself by taking on human form and submitting Himself to death on the cross. However, God exalted Him and gave Him the name that is above every name so that in the name of Jesus, every knee should bow and every tongue confess that Jesus Christ is Lord.

When believers pray in the name of Jesus Christ, they acknowledge His authority and ask God to grant their request based on Jesus' merit and not their own. They are approaching God through the sacrificial work of Jesus Christ, which gives them access to God's presence and power.

Furthermore, praying in the name of Jesus Christ means praying according to His will and character. Jesus taught His followers to pray, "Thy will be done," and so praying in His name involves aligning our petitions with God's purposes and desires.

Amen, amen, I say to you, whoever believes in me will do the works that I do, and will do greater ones than these, because I am

The biblical means of faith is a central concept in Christian theology and practice and is defined in various ways throughout the Bible. Hebrews 11:1 provides one of the most famous definitions of faith: "Now faith is the assurance of things hoped for, the conviction of things not seen." This definition highlights two key components of faith: assurance and conviction.

Assurance in this context refers to a deep sense of trust and confidence in God's promises, even when circumstances may seem uncertain or difficult. Faith means believing that God is faithful and will fulfill His promises, even when we cannot yet see the evidence of it.

Conviction, on the other hand, refers to a firm belief in the truth of God's Word and the reality of His existence. Faith involves trusting in God's character and believing that He is who He says He is, even when the world around us may seem to contradict that truth.

Hebrews 11 goes on to give numerous examples of people in the Bible who demonstrated faith through their actions. Abraham, for example, demonstrated his faith by leaving his homeland and trusting that God would provide a new home for him. Moses demonstrated his faith by leading the Israelites out of Egypt, even though he initially doubted his own abilities.

These examples highlight another key aspect of biblical faith: it is not just a matter of belief or intellectual assent but is demonstrated through action. True faith results in obedience to God's commands and a willingness to follow His lead, even when it requires us to step out of our comfort zones or face difficult circumstances.

Faith is an essential aspect of belief and practice and is highlighted in numerous passages throughout the Bible. Romans 4:17 and Genesis 15:1-6 provide insight into why faith is so important for believers.

Romans 4:17 states, "As it is written: 'I have made you a father of many nations.' He is our Father in the sight of God, in whom he believed—the God who gives life to the dead and calls into being things that were not." This passage refers to the faith of Abraham, who was promised by God that he would become the Father of many nations, even though he was initially childless and his wife was barren. Abraham's faith in God's promise was credited to him as righteousness.

Similarly, in Genesis 15:1-6, God promised Abraham that his descendants would be as numerous as the stars in the sky. Abraham believed in God's promise, and his faith was credited to him as righteousness.

These passages highlight the importance of faith as a means of receiving God's promises. As believers, we are called to have faith in God's character, His promises, and His plan for our lives. Faith allows us to trust in God's goodness and His ability to fulfill His promises, even when circumstances may seem uncertain or difficult.

Additionally, faith is essential for our salvation. Ephesians 2:8-9 states, "For it is by grace you have been saved, through faith—and this is not from yourselves, it is the gift of God—not by works so that no one can boast." Our salvation is a result of our faith in Jesus Christ and His sacrificial work on the cross.

Knowing this, that the trying of your faith worketh patience. But let patience have her perfect work, that ye may be perfect and entire, wanting nothing. If any of you lack wisdom, let him ask of God, that giveth to all men liberally, and upbraideth not; and it shall be given him. But let him ask in faith, nothing wavering. For he that wavereth is like a wave of the sea driven with the wind and tossed. For let not that man think that he shall receive any thing of the Lord. A double minded man is unstable in all his ways. James 1: 3-8

Now the just shall live by faith: but if any man draw back, my soul shall have no pleasure in him. But we are not of them who draw back unto perdition; but of them that believe to the saving of the soul. Hebrew 10:38-39

Proverbs 18:21 states, "The tongue has the power of life and death, and those who love it will eat its fruit." This verse emphasizes the significant impact that our words can have on our lives and the lives of others. It reminds us that the words we speak have the power to build up or tear down, to encourage or discourage, to heal or to hurt.

Therefore, it is essential to choose our words carefully and to use them to uplift and inspire others.

Proverbs 21:23 also speaks to the power of the tongue, stating, "Those who guard their mouths and their tongues keep themselves from calamity." This verse encourages us to be mindful of our words and to use them wisely. It reminds us that our words can have consequences and that we should strive to avoid saying things that could cause harm or damage.

When it comes to talking about faith, life, and death, it is essential to remember the power of our words. Our words can have a profound impact on those around us and can either encourage or discourage others in their faith. Therefore, we should strive to speak words of encouragement and hope, sharing the love and truth of Christ with others.

Faith in God and His word can be understood through the teachings of Romans 10:17, which states, "So then faith comes by hearing, and hearing by the word of God."

This verse suggests that faith in God and His word is built through hearing and internalizing the teachings found in the Bible. This means that as we listen to and study God's word, we begin to understand and believe in the promises and truths it contains.

Faith in God also involves trust and reliance on Him, as well as a willingness to follow His guidance and obey His commands. This trust is built through a personal relationship with God, which is strengthened through prayer and meditation on His word and living according to His will.

Faith in God and His word involves both an intellectual understanding and a personal trust in His teachings, as well as a commitment to living according to His will. It is a dynamic and ongoing process that is built through continual study, prayer, and obedience to God's word.

Matthew 11:22-24 is a passage in the New Testament where Jesus is addressing the people of Chorazin, Bethsaida, and Capernaum, three towns in the region of Galilee, and rebuking them for their lack of faith. In this passage, Jesus says:

"22 But I tell you, it will be more bearable for Tyre and Sidon on the day of judgment than for you. 23 And you, Capernaum, will you be lifted to the heavens? No, you will go down to Hades. For if the miracles that were performed in you had been performed in Sodom, they would have remained to this day. 24 But I tell you that it will be more bearable for Sodom on the day of judgment than for you."

From this passage, it is clear that Jesus is referring to the people of these towns and their lack of faith. He is saying that they have witnessed many miracles and teachings but still have not believed in him as the Messiah. Therefore, they will face a harsher judgment than even the notoriously sinful cities of Tyre, Sidon, and Sodom.

In general, the Bible teaches that faith is necessary for salvation and a right relationship with God. This faith is not just a vague belief in God's existence but a trust in Jesus Christ as Savior and Lord. It is a belief that he died for our sins, was buried, and rose again on the third day, as Paul writes in 1 Corinthians 15:3-4.

Therefore, anyone who desires to have a relationship with God needs to have faith in Jesus Christ as their Lord and Savior. This includes people of all backgrounds and walks of life, regardless of their past sins or mistakes. As Jesus says in John 3:16, "For God so loved the world that he gave his one and only Son, that whoever believes in him shall not perish but have eternal life."

For what saith the Scripture? Abraham believed God, and it was counted unto him for righteousness. Now to him that worketh is the reward not reckoned of grace, but of debt. But to him that worketh not, but believeth on him that justifieth the ungodly, his faith is counted for righteousness. Even as David also describeth the blessedness of the man, unto whom God imputeth righteousness without works, Saying, Blessed are they whose iniquities are forgiven, and whose sins are covered. Blessed is the man to whom the Lord will not impute sin. Cometh this blessedness then upon the circumcision only, or upon the uncircumcision also? for we say that faith was reckoned to Abraham for righteousness. Romans 4:3-9

Romans 1:17 says, "For in the gospel the righteousness of God is revealed—a righteousness that is by faith from first to last, just as it is written: 'The righteous will live by faith.'" This verse emphasizes that righteousness comes from faith and that the believer should live by faith. This means that faith is not just a one-time event but a way of life that should govern every aspect of the believer's life.

Similarly, Galatians 3:11 states, "Clearly no one who relies on the law is justified before God, because 'the righteous will live by faith.'" In this verse, Paul contrasts faith with relying on the law. He is saying that those who try to earn their salvation through the law will never be justified before God because salvation comes through faith in Jesus Christ.

A biblical prayer is a form of communication between human beings and God. It is an act of worship and a way to express gratitude, praise, confession, and petitions to God. Prayer is not only a means of communicating with God, but it is also an important part of building a relationship with Him.

Philippians 4:6-7 says, "Do not be anxious about anything, but in every situation, by prayer and petition, with thanksgiving, present your requests to God. And the peace of God, which transcends all understanding, will guard your hearts and your minds in Christ Jesus."

This passage highlights the importance of prayer in our lives. We are encouraged to pray about everything, including our anxieties and worries, and to do so with thanksgiving. When we bring our concerns and requests to God in prayer, we can experience the peace of God that surpasses all understanding.

Luke 18:1 says, "Then Jesus told his disciples a parable to show them that they should always pray and not give up." This verse highlights the importance of prayer and perseverance in our prayer life. Prayer is not just a one-time event or an occasional activity, but it should be a regular and consistent practice in our lives.

Prayer is a way to build and strengthen our relationship with God. Through prayer, we can communicate with Him, express our gratitude, confess our sins, and ask for guidance and help. A prayer is an act of trust in God. When we pray, we acknowledge that we are dependent on Him and that He has the power to answer our prayers.

Prayer is a source of strength and comfort in times of trouble. As we bring our concerns and requests to God in prayer, we can experience His peace and comfort, as mentioned in Philippians 4:6-7.

And he spake a parable unto them to this end, that men ought always to pray, and not to faint. Luke 18:1

Romans 1:7- 9 says, "To all those in Rome who are loved by God and called to be saints: Grace to you and peace from God our Father and the Lord Jesus Christ. First, I thank my God through Jesus Christ for all of you because your faith is proclaimed in all the world. For God is my witness, whom I serve with my spirit in the Gospel of his Son, that without ceasing I mention you."

In this passage, Paul is writing to the believers in Rome, expressing his gratitude for them and their faith.

From this, we can infer that prayer should be directed toward other believers, those who are loved by God and called to be saints.

1 Timothy 2:1-2 says, "I urge that supplications, prayers, intercessions, and thanksgivings be made for all people, for kings and all who are in high positions, that we may lead a peaceful and quiet life, godly and dignified in every way."

Matthew 5:44 says, "But I say to you, Love your enemies and pray for those who persecute you."

James 5:13-16 says, "Is anyone among you suffering? Let him pray. Is anyone cheerful? Let him sing praise...pray for one another, that you may be healed."

Philippians 4:6 says, "Do not be anxious about anything, but in everything by prayer and supplication with thanksgiving let your requests be made known to God."

Explain How should you pray glory to God? With reference to Ephesians 6: 18-20

In Ephesians 6:18-20, the Apostle Paul instructs believers to "pray in the Spirit on all occasions with all kinds of prayers and requests." This means that we should pray to God not only when we need something or when we're in trouble but also when we want to praise Him and give Him glory.

When praying to give glory to God, it is important to focus on His greatness and majesty. We can start by acknowledging His character and attributes, such as His love, mercy, grace, holiness, and sovereignty. We can also praise Him for His creation, provision, protection, and blessings in our lives.

It is important to pray in the Spirit, which means to be led by the Holy Spirit and to pray according to God's will. We should ask the Holy Spirit to help us pray and to guide our words and thoughts.

We can also use the words of Scripture to give glory to God in our prayers. For example, we can use the Psalms or other passages of Scripture to express our praise and adoration.

To magnify God is to make Him bigger and more significant in our hearts and minds, to give Him the honor and reverence He deserves, and to acknowledge His greatness and power. This is something that can be done through praise, worship, and adoration.

In Psalm 34:1-9, David magnifies God by praising Him for His goodness and mercy. He encourages others to join him in praising the Lord and testifying to His greatness. David also acknowledges his own weakness and dependence on God, which highlights God's strength and faithfulness.

Verse 3 of Psalm 34 says, "Oh, magnify the Lord with me, and let us exalt His name together." This verse shows that magnifying God is not something that we do alone but rather together with other believers. It is a communal act of worship that brings us closer to God and to one another.

In Psalm 69, David is in distress and cries out to God for help. However, even in his desperation, he magnifies God by acknowledging His power and sovereignty. David recognizes that God is his only hope and that He alone can save him from his enemies.

Verse 30 of Psalm 69 says, "I will praise the name of God with a song; I will magnify him with thanksgiving." This verse shows that even in difficult circumstances, we can magnify God through our praise and thanksgiving. It is a way to focus our hearts and minds on His goodness and to trust in His provision and care.

In Acts 10:44-46, we see an example of how the Holy Spirit can magnify God through the preaching of the Gospel. The passage describes a scene where Peter is preaching the good news about Jesus Christ to a group of Gentiles. As Peter was speaking, the Holy Spirit fell upon the Gentiles, and they began speaking in tongues and praising God.

While Peter yet spake these words, the Holy Ghost fell on all them which heard the word. And they of the circumcision which believed were astonished, as many as came with Peter, because that on the Gentiles also was poured out the gift of the Holy Ghost. For they heard them speak with tongues, and magnify God. Then answered Peter, - Acts 10: 44-46

This event demonstrates how the Holy Spirit can magnify God in a powerful and tangible way. When the Gentiles spoke in tongues, they were not speaking in their own languages but rather in languages that they had not learned. This miraculous manifestation of the Holy Spirit's power drew attention to God's greatness and sovereignty.

Additionally, the fact that the Gentiles began praising God shows how the Holy Spirit can inspire and empower us to magnify God through our worship. When we are filled with the Holy Spirit, our worship becomes more genuine and heartfelt, and we are better able to express our love and adoration for God.

Furthermore, the fact that the Gentiles were able to receive the Holy Spirit despite their non-Jewish background shows how the Gospel can magnify God's grace and mercy. The Gospel message is for all people, regardless of their race, ethnicity, or background. Through the power of the Holy Spirit, God's love and salvation can reach even the most unlikely of places and people.

Chapter Two

Prayer and Meditation for the Kingdom of God

Faith, as defined in the Bible, is a powerful and transformative concept that underlies the relationship between God and his people. At its core, faith is the belief and trust in God's promises, even when we can't see them yet. In Hebrews 11:1, the Bible tells us that "faith is the substance of things hoped for, the evidence of things not seen."

And Jesus answering saith unto them, Have faith in God. For verily I say unto you, That whosoever shall say unto this mountain, Be thou removed, and be thou cast into the sea; and shall not doubt in his heart, but shall believe that those things which he saith shall come to pass; he shall have whatsoever he saith. Therefore I say unto you, What things soever ye desire, when ye pray, believe that ye receive them, and ye shall have them. And when ye stand praying, forgive, if ye have ought against any: that your Father also which is in heaven may forgive you your trespasses. Mark 11:22-25

Faith is not just about believing in God's existence but about trusting in His character and His plan for our lives. In Romans 8:28, we are reminded that "all things work together for good to those who love God, to those who are called according to His purpose." This means that even when we face challenges or difficult circumstances, we can have faith that God is working all things for our ultimate good.

One of the most powerful examples of faith in the Bible is the story of Abraham. In Genesis 12, God tells Abraham to leave his homeland and go to a new land that he will show him. Despite not knowing where he was going, Abraham had faith in God's promises and obeyed his command. As a result, God blessed Abraham and his descendants, and he became known as the Father of faith.

Another example of faith can be found in the story of the woman who was healed by touching the hem of Jesus' garment. In Mark 5:34, Jesus tells her, "Daughter, your faith has made you well. Go in peace and be healed of your affliction." This woman had faith that even a small touch of Jesus' garment would bring healing, and her faith was rewarded.

Faith is not always easy, and it often requires us to step out of our comfort zones and trust in God's plan. But when we do, the Bible promises that we will be blessed. In Matthew 17:20, Jesus says, "If you have faith as small as a mustard seed, you can say to this mountain, 'Move from here to there,' and it will move. Nothing will be impossible for you."

Faith is a foundational concept in the Bible that requires belief, trust, and obedience to God's promises and plans. It is through faith that we can experience the blessings and miracles that God has in store for us.

Faith is a complex concept that has been debated and explored by philosophers, theologians, and scholars for centuries. In the context of Hebrews 11:1-7, faith is described as a confident assurance in what is hoped for and a conviction about things that are not seen.

Hebrews 11:1 states, "Now faith is confidence in what we hope for and assurance about what we do not see." This verse sets the tone for the rest of the passage by emphasizing the importance of having trust and belief in things that cannot be proven or seen. The concept of faith is based on the idea that there are certain things that we believe to be true, even though we cannot see them with our own eyes.

The subsequent verses in Hebrews 11 describe the examples of faith demonstrated by the heroes of the Old Testament. Abel, Enoch, Noah, Abraham, Sarah, Isaac, Jacob, and Joseph are all praised for their faith in God and their obedience to his commands. These individuals were all able to look beyond the physical world and trust in God's promises, even though they did not always fully understand what was happening around them.

And being found in fashion as a man, he humbled himself, and became obedient unto death, even the death of the cross. Wherefore God also hath highly exalted him, and given him a name which is above every name: That at the name of Jesus every knee should bow, of things in heaven, and things in earth, and things under the earth; And that every tongue should confess that Jesus Christ is Lord, to the glory of God the Father. Philippians 2:8-11

One of the key aspects of faith, as described in Hebrews 11, is that it requires action. Verse 2 states, "This is what the ancients were commended for." The faith of these Old Testament heroes was not simply a matter of belief or intellectual assent; it was demonstrated through their actions. Abel offered a sacrifice to God, Enoch walked with God, Noah built an ark, and Abraham obeyed God's command to leave his homeland and go to a place that God would show him.

Faith is not only an intellectual belief or an emotional feeling; it is also a way of life. As Hebrews 11:6 states, "And without faith, it is impossible to please God, because anyone who comes to him must believe that he exists and that he rewards those who earnestly seek him." Faith is an essential component of a relationship with God, and it is only through faith that we can truly please Him.

Faith is a confident assurance in what is hoped for and a conviction about things that are not seen. It requires action, and it is a way of life that is demonstrated through obedience to God's commands. Faith is essential for a relationship with God and is demonstrated by the heroes of the Old Testament who trusted in God's promises and acted on that trust.

Prayer is a powerful and transformative act that has been a central aspect of Christian worship for centuries. According to the Bible, prayer is a way to communicate with God and express our deepest desires, fears, and hopes.

One of the most well-known passages about prayer is Matthew 6:9-13, also known as the Lord's Prayer. In this passage, Jesus teaches his disciples how to pray, starting with the words, "Our Father in heaven, hallowed be your name." This phrase emphasizes the closeness of God and the reverence that we should have for Him.

The Lord's Prayer also includes requests for God's will to be done on earth as it is in heaven, for daily provision, for forgiveness, and for protection from temptation. Through this prayer, Jesus encourages his followers to approach God with humility, faith, and a desire to align their will with His.

Another important passage about prayer is James 5:16, which states,

"Therefore confess your sins to each other and pray for each other so that you may be healed. The prayer of a righteous person is powerful and effective."

This verse highlights the importance of confession and community in prayer. It also emphasizes the power of prayer to bring healing and transformation.

In Philippians 4:6-7, the apostle Paul writes, "Do not be anxious about anything, but in every situation, by prayer and petition, with thanksgiving, present your requests to God. And the peace of God, which transcends all understanding, will guard your hearts and your minds in Christ Jesus." This passage emphasizes the power of prayer to bring peace and calm to our lives, even in the midst of difficult circumstances.

Finally, 1 Thessalonians 5:16-18 states,

"Rejoice always, pray continually, give thanks in all circumstances; for this is God's will for you in Christ Jesus."

This verse highlights the importance of a constant attitude of prayer and gratitude in our lives, recognizing that prayer is not just a ritual or a formal act but a way of life. Prayer is a vital aspect of the Christian faith that allows us to communicate with God, express our deepest desires, and align our will with His. Through prayer, we can find peace, healing, and transformation, and we can live a life of constant gratitude and joy.

Give us this day our daily bread. And forgive us our debts, As we forgive our debtors. And do not lead us into temptation, But deliver us from the evil one. [a]For Yours is the kingdom and the power and the glory forever. Amen. Matthew 6:11-13

Matthew 6:11-13 is a part of Jesus' teaching on prayer, known as the Lord's Prayer or the Our Father. In these verses, Jesus instructs his disciples how to approach God the Father in their prayers. Let's break down the verses and understand how they emphasize the importance of remembering and approaching God the Father's name constantly through prayer and faith.

Matthew 6:11: "Give us today the food we need." This verse reminds us that we are dependent on God for our daily sustenance. By acknowledging that God provides for our physical needs, we are acknowledging His role as our Father and Provider. This verse teaches us to remember God's name as the One who provides for us and to approach Him with faith that He will continue to do so.

Matthew 6:12: "Forgive us our sins, as we have forgiven those who sin against us." This verse highlights the importance of forgiveness in our relationship with God and others. By asking God to forgive our sins, we are acknowledging His role as a merciful and gracious Father who forgives us when we repent. However, this verse also emphasizes the importance of extending forgiveness to others, just as we expect to be forgiven by God. This teaches us to approach God's name with a heart that is willing to forgive and be forgiven and to have faith in His forgiveness and grace.

Matthew 6:13: "And don't let us yield to temptation, but rescue us from the evil one." This verse acknowledges our vulnerability to temptation and evil and our need for God's protection. By asking God to deliver us from evil, we recognize His role as a powerful and loving Father who protects us from harm. This verse teaches us to approach God's name with a posture of humility and dependence, constantly seeking His help and guidance and having faith in His ability to rescue and protect us.

Matthew 6:11-13 teaches us to remember and approach God the Father's name constantly through prayer and faith, acknowledging His roles as our Provider, Forgiver, and Protector. It reminds us of our dependence on Him and the need to have a humble and trusting attitude in our prayers. By remembering and approaching God's name with faith, we deepen our relationship with Him and align our hearts with His will. This ultimately helps us grow in our faith and experience the love, grace, and protection of our heavenly Father.

So, as followers of Jesus, we are encouraged to approach God the Father with reverence, faith, and a deep understanding of His character as we pray, just as Jesus taught his disciples in Matthew 6:11-13. So, remembering and approaching God the Father's name constantly through prayer and faith is an essential aspect of our relationship with Him as our loving Father. As we do so, we can experience His presence, guidance, and blessings in our lives. It reminds us to keep God at the center of our lives and to seek His will above all else. By remembering and approaching God's name constantly through prayer and faith, we demonstrate our love, trust, and reverence for Him, and we invite His power and grace into our lives. So, let us strive to keep God's name in our hearts and minds as we approach Him in prayer, and may our faith in Him be continually strengthened. Amen. May God bless you as you seek Him in prayer and faith.

Remember, approach, and trust in God the Father's name always! Amen. May God bless you as you seek Him in prayer and faith. Remember, approach, and trust in God the Father's name always! Amen. May God bless you as you seek Him in prayer and faith. Remember, approach, and trust in

Philippians 2:8-11 describes the humility and exaltation of Jesus Christ, and how He willingly humbled Himself and became obedient to death on the cross, but was ultimately exalted to the highest place of honor by God the Father. While this passage doesn't explicitly use the word "meditation," it does offer insights into the attitude and mindset that Christians should cultivate as they reflect on the person and work of Jesus Christ.

Meditation is a spiritual discipline that involves reflecting on God's word, character, and works and seeking to internalize these truths and apply them to one's life. The Bible offers many examples of meditation, including:

Psalm 1:2: "But they delight in the law of the Lord, meditating on it day and night." This verse encourages believers to delight in God's word and to meditate on it constantly, in order to grow in their knowledge of God and in their obedience to His commands.

Psalm 119:15: "I meditate on your precepts and consider your ways." This verse highlights the importance of meditating on God's commands and ways, in order to gain insight into His character and to align one's life with His will.

Psalm 143:5: "I meditate on all your works and consider what your hands have done." This verse encourages believers to meditate on God's works and to consider the ways in which He has demonstrated His power and faithfulness, in order to strengthen their faith and trust in Him.

When we meditate on the humility and exaltation of Jesus Christ as described in Philippians 2:8-11, we can gain a deeper appreciation for His sacrificial love and can be inspired to imitate His humility and obedience in our own lives. We can also be reminded of the ultimate victory that Christ has won over sin and death and can find hope and encouragement in His triumph. Through meditation on God's word and on the person and work of Jesus Christ, we can grow in our faith, deepen our relationship with God, and experience the transforming power of His grace in our lives.

In the book of Joshua, we see a fascinating example of meditation in action in the story of the conquest of the city of Ai. After the Israelites were defeated in their first attempt to take the city, Joshua and the elders of Israel fell on their faces before God, seeking His wisdom and guidance (Joshua 7:6-9). Through this posture of humble dependence and prayerful reflection, Joshua received insight from God that ultimately led to victory over Ai.

This example illustrates several key elements of meditation that are relevant to us today:

Humility: Like Joshua and the Israelites, true meditation requires a posture of humility and dependence on God. We must recognize our own limitations and inadequacies and acknowledge our need for divine wisdom and guidance.

Reflection: Meditation involves reflecting deeply on God's word, character, and works, seeking to gain insight and understanding that can inform our actions and attitudes.

Prayer: Meditation is not merely an intellectual exercise but also a spiritual discipline that involves prayerful communication with God. As we meditate on His word and seek His guidance, we must also be open to His leading and responsive to His promptings.

In the story of Ai, we see how these elements of meditation came together in a powerful way to bring about victory for the Israelites. Through their posture of humble dependence, their reflection on God's word and character, and their prayerful communication with Him, they were able to discern His will and act on it with confidence and courage.

As we seek to cultivate a practice of meditation in our own lives, we can learn from this example and apply these same principles. Whether we are facing challenges and obstacles like the Israelites or simply seeking to grow in our relationship with God, meditation can be a powerful tool for deepening our faith, strengthening our resolve, and discerning God's will for our lives.

In the name of the Father, the Son, and the Holy Ghost, be exalted in the kingdom of God this day through those who are called to be apostles through the spirit of the living God, by faith in Jesus' name.

In the name of the Father, the Son, and the Holy Ghost, be exalted in the kingdom of God this day through those that are called to be prophets through the spirit of the living God, by faith in Jesus' name.

In the name of the Father, the Son, and the Holy Ghost, be exalted in the kingdom of God this day through those who are called to be evangelists through the spirit of the living God, by faith in Jesus' name.

In the name of the Father, the Son, and the Holy Ghost, be exalted in the kingdom of God this day through those who are called to be pastors through the spirit of the living God, by faith in Jesus' name.

In the name of the Father, the Son, and the Holy Ghost, be exalted in the kingdom of God this day through those who are called to be teachers through the spirit of the living God, by faith in Jesus' name.

In the name of the Father, the Son, and the Holy Ghost, be exalted in the kingdom of God this day through those that are called no weapon form shall prosper through the spirit of the living God, by faith in Jesus' name.

In the name of the Father, the Son, and the Holy Ghost, be exalted in the kingdom of God this day through those who are called to put on the whole armor of God through the spirit of the living God, by faith in Jesus' name.

In the name of the Father, the Son, and the Holy Ghost, be exalted in the kingdom of God this day through those that are called to be blameless under the coming of our Lord Jesus' name through the spirit of the living God, by faith in Jesus' name.

In the name of the Father, the Son, and the Holy Ghost,
be exalted in the kingdom of God this day through those
who are called to walk by faith and not by sight through
the spirit of the living God, by faith in Jesus' name.

In the name of the Father, the Son, and the Holy Ghost,
be exalted in the kingdom of God this day through those
that are called to be sanctified holy through the spirit of
the living God, by faith in Jesus' name.

In the name of the Father, the Son, and the Holy Ghost,
be exalted in the kingdom of God this day through those
that are called to be filled with the Holy Ghost and fire
through the spirit of the living God, by faith in Jesus'
name.

In the name of the Father, the Son, and the Holy Ghost,
be exalted in the kingdom of God this day through those
who are called to pray without ceasing through the spirit
of the living God, by faith in Jesus' name.

In the name of the Father, the Son, and the Holy Ghost,
be exalted in the kingdom of God this day through those
who are called to have the power to heal the sick, cleanse
the leper, and raise the dead through the spirit of the
living God, by faith in Jesus' name.

In the name of the Father, the Son, and the Holy Ghost, be exalted in the kingdom of God this day to live in obedience through the spirit of the living God, by faith in Jesus' name.

In the name of the Father, the Son, and the Holy Ghost, be exalted in the kingdom of God this day through those who are called to restore Christ's name through the spirit of the living God, by faith in Jesus' name.

In the name of the Father, the Son, and the Holy Ghost, be exalted in the kingdom of God this day through those who are called to go into all the world to preach the gospel through the spirit of the living God, by faith in Jesus' name.

In the name of the Father, the Son, and the Holy Ghost, be exalted in the kingdom of God this day through those who are called to have the power to get wealth through the spirit of the living God, by faith in Jesus' name.

In the name of the Father, the Son, and the Holy Ghost, be exalted in the kingdom of God this day through those who are called to root up, tear down, and plant through the spirit of the living God, by faith in Jesus' name.

In the name of the Father, the Son, and the Holy Ghost,
be exalted in the kingdom of God this day through those
who are called to walk by faith and not by spite through
the spirit of the living God, by faith in Jesus' name.

In the name of the Father, the Son, and the Holy Ghost,
be exalted in the kingdom of God this day through those
who are called to maintain the fire of the Holy Ghost
through the spirit of the living God, by faith in Jesus'
name.

In the name of the Father, the Son, and the Holy Ghost,
be exalted in the kingdom of God this day through those
who are called to spread the love of God in their hearts
by the Holy God through the spirit of the living God, by
faith in Jesus' name.

In the name of the Father, the Son, and the Holy Ghost,
be exalted in the kingdom of God this day through those
who are called to bring into captivity every thought to
the obedience of Christ through the spirit of the living
God, by faith in Jesus' name.

In the name of the Father, the Son, and the Holy Ghost,
be exalted in the kingdom of God this day through those
that are called to flow in the fruit of the spirit through
the spirit of the living God, by faith in Jesus' name.

In the name of the Father, the Son, and the Holy Ghost, be exalted in the kingdom of God this day through those who are called to manifest the love of God through the spirit of the living God, by faith in Jesus' name.

In the name of the Father, the Son, and the Holy Ghost, be exalted in the kingdom of God this day through those who are called to hold onto Jesus Christ, the author and the finisher of their faith through the spirit of the living God, by faith in Jesus' name.

Chapter Three
Prayer Meditation for Yourself

In the name of the Father, the Son, and the Holy Ghost, be supreme in my being this day; I am the redeemed of the Lord through the spirit of the living God, by faith in Jesus' name.

In the name of the Father, the Son, and the Holy Ghost, be supreme in my being this day; I am what I am by the grace of the Lord through the spirit of the living God, by faith in Jesus' name.

In the name of the Father, the Son, and the Holy Ghost, be supreme in my being this day; I am the repentance of the Lord through the spirit of the living God, by faith in Jesus Christ.

In the name of the Father, the Son, and the Holy Ghost, be supreme in my being this day; I am the righteousness of the Lord through the spirit of the living God, by faith in Jesus' name.

In the name of the Father, the Son, and the Holy Ghost, be supreme in my being this day; I am the forgiveness of

the Lord through the spirit of the living God, by faith in
Jesus' name.

In the name of the Father, the Son, and the Holy Ghost,
be supreme in my being this day; I am the justification of
the Lord through the spirit of the living God, by faith in
Jesus' name.

In the name of the Father, the Son, and the Holy Ghost,
be supreme in my being this day; I am the power to get
the wealth of the Lord through the spirit of the living
God, by faith in Jesus' name.

In the name of the Father, the Son, and the Holy Ghost,
be supreme in my being this day; I am the fire baptized
of the Lord through the spirit of the living God, by faith
in Jesus' name.

In the name of the Father, the Son, and the Holy Ghost,
be supreme in my being this day; I am the fruit of the
spirit of the Lord through the spirit of the living God, by
faith in Jesus' name.

In the name of the Father, the Son, and the Holy Ghost,
be supreme in my being this day; I am the gift of the

spirit of the Lord through the spirit of the living God, by faith in Jesus' name.

In the name of the Father, the Son, and the Holy Ghost, be supreme in my being this day; I am the blessed going out and the blessed coming in of the Lord through the spirit of the living God by faith in Jesus' name.

In the name of the Father, the Son, and the Holy Ghost, be supreme in my being this day; I am the healing mercy of the Lord through the spirit of the living God, by faith in Jesus' name.

In the name of the Father, the Son, and the Holy Ghost, be supreme in my being this day; I am the divine protection of the Lord through the spirit of the living God, by faith in Jesus' name.

In the name of the Father, the Son, and the Holy Ghost, be supreme in my being this day; I am the friend that sticketh closer than a brother of the Lord through the spirit of the living God, by faith in Jesus' name.

In the name of the Father, the Son, and the Holy Ghost, be supreme in my being this day; I am the apostle of the

Lord through the spirit of the living God, by faith in
Jesus' name.

In the name of the Father, the Son, and the Holy Ghost,
be supreme in my being this day; I am the prophet of the
Lord through the spirit of the living God, by faith in
Jesus' name.

In the name of the Father, the Son, and the Holy Ghost,
be supreme in my being this day; I am the evangelist of
the Lord through the spirit of the living God, by faith in
Jesus' name.

In the name of the Father, the Son, and the Holy Ghost,
be supreme in my being this day; I am the pastor of the
Lord through the spirit of the living God, by faith in
Jesus' name.

In the name of the Father, the Son, and the Holy Ghost,
be supreme in my being this day; I am the teacher of the
Lord through the spirit of the living God, by faith in
Jesus' name.

In the name of the Father, the Son, and the Holy Ghost,
be supreme in my being this day; I am the prayer warrior

of the Lord through the spirit of the living God, by faith
in Jesus' name.

In the name of the Father, the Son, and the Holy Ghost,
be supreme in my being this day; I am the peacemaker of
the Lord in my home through the spirit of the living
God, by faith in Jesus' name.

In the name of the Father, the Son, and the Holy Ghost,
be supreme in my being this day; I am the example of
my children of the Lord through the spirit of the living
God, by faith in Jesus' name.

In the name of the Father, the Son, and the Holy Ghost,
be supreme in my being this day; I am the seal of the
Lord through the spirit of the living God, by faith in
Jesus' name.

In the name of the Father, the Son, and the Holy Ghost,
be supreme in my being this day; I am the entrepreneur
of the Lord through the spirit of the living God, by faith
in Jesus' name.

In the name of the Father, the Son, and the Holy Ghost,
be supreme in my being this day; I am the lover of my

wife of the Lord through the spirit of the living God, by faith in Jesus' name.

In the name of the Father, the Son, and the Holy Ghost be supreme in my being this day; I am the revelation of the things to come of the Lord through the spirit of the living God, by faith in Jesus' name.

Chapter Four

Speaking the Word of God Over Your Family

In the name of the Father, the Son, and the Holy Ghost, be glorified in my family's life this day; they are the redeemed of the Lord through the spirit of the living God, by faith in Jesus' name.

In the name of the Father, the Son, and the Holy Ghost, be glorified in my family's life this day; they are the holiness of the Lord through the spirit of the living God, by faith in Jesus' name.

In the name of the Father, the Son, and the Holy Ghost, be glorified in my family's life this day; they are the righteousness of the Lord through the spirit of the living God, by faith in Jesus' name.

In the name of the Father, the Son, and the Holy Ghost, be glorified in my family's life this day; they are the anointed of the Lord through the spirit of the living God, by faith in Jesus' name.

In the name of the Father, the Son, and the Holy Ghost, be glorified in my family's life this day; they are the sanctifications of the Lord through the spirit of the living God, by faith in Jesus' name.

In the name of the Father, the Son, and the Holy Ghost, be glorified in my family's life this day; they are the deliverance of the Lord through the spirit of the living God, by faith in Jesus' name.

In the name of the Father, the Son, and the Holy Ghost, be glorified in my family's life this day; they are the victory of the Lord through the spirit of the living God, by faith in Jesus' name.

In the name of the Father, the Son, and the Holy Ghost, be glorified in my family's life this day; they are blessed by the Lord through the spirit of the living God, by faith in Jesus' name.

In the name of the Father, the Son, and the Holy Ghost, be glorified in my family's life this day; they are the favor of the Lord through the spirit of the living God, by faith in Jesus' name.

In the name of the Father, the Son, and the Holy Ghost,
be glorified in my family's life this day; they are the
mercy of the Lord through the spirit of the living God,
by faith in Jesus' name.

In the name of the Father, the Son, and the Holy Ghost,
be glorified in my family's life this day; they are the
passion of the Lord through the spirit of the living God,
by faith in Jesus' name.

In the name of the Father, the Son, and the Holy Ghost,
be glorified in my family's life this day; they are the
oneness of the Lord through the spirit of the living God,
by faith in Jesus' name.

In the name of the Father, the Son, and the Holy Ghost,
be glorified in my family's life this day; they are the
salvation of the Lord through the spirit of the living
God, by faith in Jesus' name.

In the name of the Father, the Son, and the Holy Ghost,
be glorified in my family's life this day; they are the
compassion of the Lord through the spirit of the living
God, by faith in Jesus' name.

In the name of the Father, the Son, and the Holy Ghost,
be glorified in my family's life this day; they are the glory
of the Lord through the spirit of the living God, by faith
in Jesus' name.

In the name of the Father, the Son, and the Holy Ghost,
be glorified in my family's life this day; they are the head
and not the tail of the Lord through the spirit of the
living God, by faith in Jesus' name.

In the name of the Father, the Son, and the Holy Ghost,
be glorified in my family's life this day; they are lenders
and not the borrowers of the Lord through the spirit of
the living God, by faith in Jesus' name.

In the name of the Father, the Son, and the Holy Ghost,
be glorified in my family's life this day; they are the Holy
Ghost fire baptized of the Lord through the spirit of the
living God, by faith in Jesus' name.

In the name of the Father, the Son, and the Holy Ghost,
be glorified in my family's life this day; they are the
wisdom of the Lord through the spirit of the living God,
by faith in Jesus' name.

In the name of the Father, the Son, and the Holy Ghost, be glorified in my family's life this day; they are the blessed going out and the blessed coming in of the Lord through the spirit of the living God, by faith in Jesus' name.

In the name of the Father, the Son, and the Holy Ghost, be glorified in my family's life this day; they are the loved of the Lord through the spirit of the living God, by faith in Jesus' name.

In the name of the Father, the Son, and the Holy Ghost, be glorified in my family's life this day; they are the joy of the Lord through the spirit of the living God, by faith in Jesus' name.

In the name of the Father, the Son, and the Holy Ghost, be glorified in my family's life this day; they are the peace of the Lord through the spirit of the living God, by faith in Jesus' name.

In the name of the Father, the Son, and the Holy Ghost, be glorified in my family's life this day; they are the long-suffering of the Lord through the spirit of the living God, by faith in Jesus' name.

In the name of the Father, the Son, and the Holy Ghost,
be glorified in my family's life this day; they are the
gentleness of the Lord through the spirit of the living
God, by faith in Jesus' name.

In the name of the Father, the Son, and the Holy Ghost,
be glorified in my family's life this day; they are the faith
of the Lord through the spirit of the living God, by faith
in Jesus' name.

In the name of the Father, the Son, and the Holy Ghost,
be glorified in my family's life this day; they are the
meekness of the Lord through the spirit of the living
God, by faith in Jesus' name.

In the name of the Father, the Son, and the Holy Ghost,
be glorified in my family's life this day; they are the
temperance of the Lord through the spirit of the living
God, by faith in Jesus' name.

Chapter Five

Prayer Meditation for My Parents

In the name of the Father, the Son, and the Holy Ghost, be sanctified in my parents' mind this day; they are the redeemed of the Lord through the spirit of the living God, by faith in Jesus's name.

In the name of the Father, the Son, and the Holy Ghost, be sanctified in my parent's minds this day; they are the saints of the Most High God through the spirit of the living God, by faith in Jesus' name.

In the name of the Father, the Son, and the Holy Ghost, be sanctified in my parent's minds this day; they are the apples of God's eyes through the spirit of the living God, by faith in Jesus' name.

In the name of the Father, the Son, and the Holy Ghost, be sanctified in my parent's minds this day; they are the chosen vessels of the Lord through the spirit of the living God, by faith in Jesus' name.

In the name of the Father, the Son, and the Holy Ghost, be sanctified in my parent's minds this day; they are the

unity of God's grace through the spirit of the living God,
by faith in Jesus' name.

In the name of the Father, the Son, and the Holy Ghost,
be sanctified in my parent's minds this day; they are the
precepts of God's love through the spirit of the living
God, by faith in Jesus' name.

In the name of the Father, the Son, and the Holy Ghost,
be sanctified in my parent's minds this day; they are the
righteousness of God's glory through the spirit of the
living God, by faith in Jesus' name.

In the name of the Father, the Son, and the Holy Ghost,
be sanctified in my parent's minds this day; they are the
miracles of God's favor through the spirit of the living
God, by faith in Jesus' name.

In the name of the Father, the Son, and the Holy Ghost,
be sanctified in my parent's minds this day; they are the
joy of God's mighty through the spirit of the living God,
by faith in Jesus' name.

In the name of the Father, the Son, and the Holy Ghost,
be sanctified in my parent's minds this day; they are the

wisdom of God's power through the spirit of the living God, by faith in Jesus' name.

In the name of the Father, the Son, and the Holy Ghost, be sanctified in my parent's minds this day; they are blessed by God's goodness through the spirit of the living God, by faith in Jesus' name.

In the name of the Father, the Son, and the Holy Ghost, be sanctified in my parent's minds this day; they are the cause of God's grace through the spirit of the living God, by faith in Jesus' name.

In the name of the Father, the Son, and the Holy Ghost, be sanctified in my parent's minds this day; they are the unity of God's strength through the spirit of the living God, by faith in Jesus' name.

In the name of the Father, the Son, and the Holy Ghost, be sanctified in my parent's minds this day; they are the mind of God's understanding through the spirit of the living God, by faith in Jesus' name.

In the name of the Father, the Son, and the Holy Ghost, be sanctified in my parent's minds this day; they are the

anointing of God's truth through the spirit of the living God, by faith in Jesus' name.

In the name of the Father, the Son, and the Holy Ghost, be sanctified in my parent's minds this day; they are the examples of God's kindness through the spirit of the living God, by faith in Jesus' name.

In the name of the Father, the Son, and the Holy Ghost, be sanctified in my parent's minds this day; they are the unity of God's strength through the spirit of the living God, by faith in Jesus' name.

In the name of the Father, the Son, and the Holy Ghost, be sanctified in my parent's minds this day; they are the attractions of God's finances through the spirit of the living God, by faith in Jesus' name.

In the name of the Father, the Son, and the Holy Ghost, be sanctified in my parent's mind this day; they are the fire baptized of God's healing power through the spirit of the living God, by faith in Jesus' name.

In the name of the Father, the Son, and the Holy Ghost, be sanctified in my parent's minds this day; they are the

focus of God's mercy through the spirit of the living
God, by faith in Jesus' name.

In the name of the Father, the Son, and the Holy Ghost,
be sanctified in my parent's minds this day; they are the
teacher of God's holy word through the spirit of the
living God, by faith in Jesus' name.

In the name of the Father, the Son, and the Holy Ghost,
be sanctified in my parent's minds this day; they are the
signs and wonders of God's victory through the spirit of
the living God, by faith in Jesus' name.

In the name of the Father, the Son, and the Holy Ghost,
be sanctified in my parent's minds this day; they are the
forgiveness of God's passion through the spirit of the
living God, by faith in Jesus' name.

In the name of the Father, the Son, and the Holy Ghost,
be sanctified in my parent's minds this day; they are the
leaders of God's overflowing blessings through the spirit
of the living God, by faith in Jesus' name.

In the name of the Father, the Son, and the Holy Ghost,
be sanctified in my parent's minds this day; they are the

light of God's redemption through the spirit of the living God, by faith in Jesus' name.

In the name of the Father, the Son, and the Holy Ghost, be sanctified in my parent's minds this day; they are the meekness of God's spirit through the spirit of the living God, by faith in Jesus' name.

In the name of the Father, the Son, and the Holy Ghost, be sanctified in my parent's minds this day; they are the temperance of God's fruits through the spirit of the living God, by faith in Jesus' name.

In the name of the Father, the Son, and the Holy Ghost, be sanctified in my parent's minds this day; they are the children of God's salvation power through the spirit of the living God, by faith in Jesus' name.

Chapter Six

Speaking the Word of God Over Your Husband

In the name of the Father, the Son, and the Holy Ghost, be praised in my husband's soul this day; he is the priest and the prophet of our home through the spirit of the living God, by faith in Jesus's name.

In the name of the Father, the Son, and the Holy Ghost, be praised in my husband's soul this day; he is the redeemed of the Lord through the spirit of the living God, by faith in Jesus's name.

In the name of the Father, the Son, and the Holy Ghost, be praised in my husband's soul this day; he is the holiness of the Lord through the spirit of the living God, by faith in Jesus's name.

In the name of the Father, the Son, and the Holy Ghost, be praised in my husband's soul this day; he is the grace of the Lord through the spirit of the living God, by faith in Jesus's name.

In the name of the Father, the Son, and the Holy Ghost, be praised in my husband's soul this day; he is the salvation of the Lord through the spirit of the living God, by faith in Jesus's name.

In the name of the Father, the Son, and the Holy Ghost, be praised in my husband's soul this day; he is the mighty of the Lord through the spirit of the living God, by faith in Jesus's name.

In the name of the Father, the Son, and the Holy Ghost, be praised in my husband's soul this day; he is the anointed of the Lord through the spirit of the living God, by faith in Jesus's name.

In the name of the Father, the Son, and the Holy Ghost, be praised in my husband's soul this day; he is the righteousness of the Lord through the spirit of the living God, by faith in Jesus's name.

In the name of the Father, the Son, and the Holy Ghost, be praised in my husband's soul this day; he is the sanctification of the Lord through the spirit of the living God, by faith in Jesus's name.

In the name of the Father, the Son, and the Holy Ghost,
be praised in my husband's soul this day; he is the
compassion of the Lord through the spirit of the living
God, by faith in Jesus's name.

In the name of the Father, the Son, and the Holy Ghost,
be praised in my husband's soul this day; he is the love
of the Lord through the spirit of the living God, by faith
in Jesus's name.

In the name of the Father, the Son, and the Holy Ghost,
be praised in my husband's soul this day; he is the joy of
the Lord through the spirit of the living God, by faith in
Jesus's name.

In the name of the Father, the Son, and the Holy Ghost,
be praised in my husband's soul this day; he is the peace
of the Lord through the spirit of the living God, by faith
in Jesus's name.

In the name of the Father, the Son, and the Holy Ghost,
be praised in my husband's soul this day; he is the long-
suffering of the Lord through the spirit of the living
God, by faith in Jesus's name.

In the name of the Father, the Son, and the Holy Ghost,
be praised in my husband's soul this day; he is the
gentleness of the Lord through the spirit of the living
God, by faith in Jesus's name.

In the name of the Father, the Son, and the Holy Ghost,
be praised in my husband's soul this day; he is the
goodness of the Lord through the spirit of the living
God, by faith in Jesus's name.

In the name of the Father, the Son, and the Holy Ghost,
be praised in my husband's soul this day; he is the faith
of the Lord through the spirit of the living God, by faith
in Jesus's name.

In the name of the Father, the Son, and the Holy Ghost,
be praised in my husband's soul this day; he is the
meekness of the Lord through the spirit of the living
God, by faith in Jesus's name.

In the name of the Father, the Son, and the Holy Ghost,
be praised in my husband's soul this day; he is the
temperance of the Lord through the spirit of the living
God, by faith in Jesus's name.

In the name of the Father, the Son, and the Holy Ghost,
be praised in my husband's soul this day; he is the Holy
Ghost fire baptized of the Lord through the spirit of the
living God, by faith in Jesus's name.

In the name of the Father, the Son, and the Holy Ghost,
be praised in my husband's soul this day; he is the
wisdom of the Lord through the spirit of the living God,
by faith in Jesus's name.

In the name of the Father, the Son, and the Holy Ghost,
be praised in my husband's soul this day; he is the
knowledge of the Lord through the spirit of the living
God, by faith in Jesus's name.

In the name of the Father, the Son, and the Holy Ghost,
be praised in my husband's soul this day; he is the
understanding of the Lord through the spirit of the
living God, by faith in Jesus's name.

In the name of the Father, the Son, and the Holy Ghost,
be praised in my husband's soul this day; he is the
resurrection of the Lord through the spirit of the living
God, by faith in Jesus's name.

In the name of the Father, the Son, and the Holy Ghost,
be praised in my husband's soul this day; he is the
miracle of the Lord through the spirit of the living God,
by faith in Jesus's name.

In the name of the Father, the Son, and the Holy Ghost,
be praised in my husband's soul this day; he is the
healing of the Lord through the spirit of the living God,
by faith in Jesus's name.

In the name of the Father, the Son, and the Holy Ghost,
be praised in my husband's soul this day; he is the voice
of the Lord through the spirit of the living God, by faith
in Jesus's name.

In the name of the Father, the Son, and the Holy Ghost,
be praised in my husband's soul this day; he is the
interpretation of the Lord through the spirit of the living
God, by faith in Jesus's name.

In the name of the Father, the Son, and the Holy Ghost,
be praised in my husband's soul this day; he is the head
and not the tail of the Lord through the spirit of the
living God, by faith in Jesus's name.

Chapter Seven

Speaking the Word of God Over Your Wife

In the name of the Father, the Son, and the Holy Ghost, be exalted in my wife's heart this day; she is the 31 Proverbs woman of our home, through the spirit of the living God, by faith in Jesus's name.

In the name of the Father, the Son, and the Holy Ghost, be exalted in my wife's heart this day; she is the redeemed of the Lord through the spirit of the living God, by faith in Jesus's name.

In the name of the Father, the Son, and the Holy Ghost, be exalted in my wife's heart this day; she is the peace of the Lord through the spirit of the living God, by faith in Jesus's name.

In the name of the Father, the Son, and the Holy Ghost, be exalted in my wife's heart this day; she is the righteousness of the Lord through the spirit of the living God, by faith in Jesus's name.

In the name of the Father, the Son, and the Holy Ghost,
be exalted in my wife's heart this day; she is the mighty
of the Lord through the spirit of the living God, by faith
in Jesus's name.

In the name of the Father, the Son, and the Holy Ghost,
be exalted in my wife's heart this day; she is the servant
of the Lord through the spirit of the living God, by faith
in Jesus's name.

In the name of the Father, the Son, and the Holy Ghost,
be exalted in my wife's heart this day; she is the holiness
of the Lord through the spirit of the living God, by faith
in Jesus's name.

In the name of the Father, the Son, and the Holy Ghost,
be exalted in my wife's heart this day; she is the salvation
of the Lord through the spirit of the living God, by faith
in Jesus's name.

In the name of the Father, the Son, and the Holy Ghost,
be exalted in my wife's heart this day; she is the passion
of the Lord through the spirit of the living God, by faith
in Jesus's name.

In the name of the Father, the Son, and the Holy Ghost, be exalted in my wife's heart this day; she is the compassion of the Lord through the spirit of the living God, by faith in Jesus's name.

In the name of the Father, the Son, and the Holy Ghost, be exalted in my wife's heart this day; she is the wonder of the Lord through the spirit of the living God, by faith in Jesus's name.

In the name of the Father, the Son, and the Holy Ghost, be exalted in my wife's heart this day; she is the goodwill of the Lord through the spirit of the living God, by faith in Jesus's name.

In the name of the Father, the Son, and the Holy Ghost, be exalted in my wife's heart this day; she is the temperance of the Lord through the spirit of the living God, by faith in Jesus's name.

In the name of the Father, the Son, and the Holy Ghost, be exalted in my wife's heart this day; she is the gentleness of the Lord through the spirit of the living God, by faith in Jesus's name.

In the name of the Father, the Son, and the Holy Ghost, be exalted in my wife's heart this day; she is the - sanctification of the Lord through the spirit of the living God, by faith in Jesus's name.

In the name of the Father, the Son, and the Holy Ghost, be exalted in my wife's heart this day; she is the grace of the Lord through the spirit of the living God, by faith in Jesus's name.

In the name of the Father, the Son, and the Holy Ghost, be exalted in my wife's heart this day; she is the kindness of the Lord through the spirit of the living God, by faith in Jesus's name.

In the name of the Father, the Son, and the Holy Ghost, be exalted in my wife's heart this day; she is the justification of the Lord through the spirit of the living God, by faith in Jesus's name.

In the name of the Father, the Son, and the Holy Ghost, be exalted in my wife's heart this day; she is the Holy Ghost baptized of the Lord through the spirit of the living God, by faith in Jesus's name.

In the name of the Father, the Son, and the Holy Ghost, be exalted in my wife's heart this day; she is the good keeper at the home of the Lord through the spirit of the living God, by faith in Jesus's name.

In the name of the Father, the Son, and the Holy Ghost, be exalted in my wife's heart this day; she is the woman of the Lord through the spirit of the living God, by faith in Jesus's name.

In the name of the Father, the Son, and the Holy Ghost, be exalted in my wife's heart this day; she is the testimony of the Lord through the spirit of the living God, by faith in Jesus's name.

In the name of the Father, the Son, and the Holy Ghost, be exalted in my wife's heart this day; she is the reflection of the love of the Lord through the spirit of the living God, by faith in Jesus's name.

In the name of the Father, the Son, and the Holy Ghost, be exalted in my wife's heart this day; she is the woman that walks by faith of the Lord through the spirit of the living God, by faith in Jesus's name.

In the name of the Father, the Son, and the Holy Ghost, be exalted in my wife's heart this day; she is the woman who really loves the Lord through the spirit of the living God, by faith in Jesus's name.

In the name of the Father, the Son, and the Holy Ghost, be exalted in my wife's heart this day; she is the woman with a meek and quiet spirit of the Lord through the spirit of the living God, by faith in Jesus's name.

Chapter Eight

Speaking the Word of God Over Our Children

In the name of the Father, the Son, and the Holy Ghost, be acknowledged in my children's spirit this day; they are the redeemed of the Lord through the spirit of the living God, by faith in Jesus's name.

In the name of the Father, the Son, and the Holy Ghost, be acknowledged in my children's spirit this day; they are the children of the Most High Lord through the spirit of the living God, by faith in Jesus's name.

In the name of the Father, the Son, and the Holy Ghost, be acknowledged in my children's spirit this day; they are the workmanship of the Lord through the spirit of the living God, by faith in Jesus's name.

In the name of the Father, the Son, and the Holy Ghost, be acknowledged in my children's spirit this day; they are the temples of the Lord through the spirit of the living God, by faith in Jesus's name.

In the name of the Father, the Son, and the Holy Ghost,
be acknowledged in my children's spirit this day; they are
the anointed of the Lord through the spirit of the living
God, by faith in Jesus's name.

In the name of the Father, the Son, and the Holy Ghost,
be acknowledged in my children's spirit this day; they are
the glory of the Lord through the spirit of the living
God, by faith in Jesus's name.

In the name of the Father, the Son, and the Holy Ghost,
be acknowledged in my children's spirit this day; they are
the mercy of the Lord through the spirit of the living
God, by faith in Jesus's name.

In the name of the Father, the Son, and the Holy Ghost,
be acknowledged in my children's spirit this day; they are
the saints of the Most High God through the spirit of
the living God, by faith in Jesus's name.

In the name of the Father, the Son, and the Holy Ghost,
be acknowledged in my children's spirit this day; they are
the servants of the Lord through the spirit of the living
God, by faith in Jesus's name.

In the name of the Father, the Son, and the Holy Ghost, be acknowledged in my children's spirit this day; they are the righteousness of the Lord through the spirit of the living God, by faith in Jesus's name.

In the name of the Father, the Son, and the Holy Ghost, be acknowledged in my children's spirit this day; they are the holiness of the Lord through the spirit of the living God, by faith in Jesus's name.

In the name of the Father, the Son, and the Holy Ghost, be acknowledged in my children's spirit this day; they are the joy of the Lord through the spirit of the living God, by faith in Jesus's name.

In the name of the Father, the Son, and the Holy Ghost, be acknowledged in my children's spirit this day; they are the power and dominion of the Lord through the spirit of the living God, by faith in Jesus's name.

In the name of the Father, the Son, and the Holy Ghost, be acknowledged in my children's spirit this day; they are the long-suffering of the Lord through the spirit of the living God, by faith in Jesus's name.

In the name of the Father, the Son, and the Holy Ghost,
be acknowledged in my children's spirit this day; they are
the peace of the Lord through the spirit of the living
God, by faith in Jesus's name.

In the name of the Father, the Son, and the Holy Ghost,
be acknowledged in my children's spirit this day; they are
the compassion of the Lord through the spirit of the
living God, by faith in Jesus's name.

In the name of the Father, the Son, and the Holy Ghost,
be acknowledged in my children's spirit this day; they are
the Holy Ghost Fire Baptized of the Lord through the
spirit of the living God, by faith in Jesus's name.

In the name of the Father, the Son, and the Holy Ghost,
be acknowledged in my children's spirit this day; they are
the blessed, blessed, blessed of the Lord through the
spirit of the living God, by faith in Jesus's name.

In the name of the Father, the Son, and the Holy Ghost,
be acknowledged in my children's spirit this day; they are
the armies of the Lord through the spirit of the living
God, by faith in Jesus's name.

In the name of the Father, the Son, and the Holy Ghost,
be acknowledged in my children's spirit this day; they are
the properties of the Lord through the spirit of the living
God, by faith in Jesus's name.

In the name of the Father, the Son, and the Holy Ghost,
be acknowledged in my children's spirit this day; they are
the financial wealth of the Lord through the spirit of the
living God, by faith in Jesus's name.

In the name of the Father, the Son, and the Holy Ghost,
be acknowledged in my children's spirit this day; they are
the salvation of the Lord through the spirit of the living
God, by faith in Jesus's name.

In the name of the Father, the Son, and the Holy Ghost,
be acknowledged in my children's spirit this day; they are
the prophets of the Lord through the spirit of the living
God, by faith in Jesus's name.

In the name of the Father, the Son, and the Holy Ghost,
be acknowledged in my children's spirit this day; they are
the wisdom of the Lord through the spirit of the living
God, by faith in Jesus's name.

In the name of the Father, the Son, and the Holy Ghost,
be acknowledged in my children's spirit this day; they are
the truth of the Lord through the spirit of the living
God, by faith in Jesus's name.

In the name of the Father, the Son, and the Holy Ghost,
be acknowledged in my children's spirit this day; they are
the miracles of the Lord through the spirit of the living
God, by faith in Jesus's name.

In the name of the Father, the Son, and the Holy Ghost,
be acknowledged in my children's spirit this day; they are
the sanctified of the Lord through the spirit of the living
God, by faith in Jesus's name.

Chapter Nine

Speaking the Word of God Over My Brothers

In the name of the Father, the Son, and the Holy Ghost, be manifested in my brother's character this day, the saving grace of the Lord through the spirit of the living God, by faith in Jesus's name.

In the name of the Father, the Son, and the Holy Ghost, be manifested in my brother's character this day, the Baptism of the Holy Ghost through the spirit of the living God, by faith in Jesus's name.

In the name of the Father, the Son, and the Holy Ghost, be manifested in my brother's character this day, the redemption of the Lord through the spirit of the living God, by faith in Jesus's name.

In the name of the Father, the Son, and the Holy Ghost, be manifested in my brother's character this day, the spirit of sanctification of the Lord through the spirit of the living God, by faith in Jesus's name.

In the name of the Father, the Son, and the Holy Ghost,
be manifested in my brother's character this day, the
steps of the Lord through the spirit of the living God, by
faith in Jesus's name.

In the name of the Father, the Son, and the Holy Ghost,
be manifested in my brother's character this day, the
commandments of the Lord through the spirit of the
living God, by faith in Jesus's name.

In the name of the Father, the Son, and the Holy Ghost,
be manifested in my brother's character this day, the
victory of the Lord through the spirit of the living God,
by faith in Jesus's name.

In the name of the Father, the Son, and the Holy Ghost,
be manifested in my brother's character this day, the
meditation of the Lord through the spirit of the living
God, by faith in Jesus's name.

In the name of the Father, the Son, and the Holy Ghost,
be manifested in my brother's character this day, the
peace of the Lord through the spirit of the living God,
by faith in Jesus's name.

In the name of the Father, the Son, and the Holy Ghost, be manifested in my brother's character this day, the justification of the Lord through the spirit of the living God, by faith in Jesus's name.

In the name of the Father, the Son, and the Holy Ghost, be manifested in my brother's character this day, the wisdom of eternal life of the Lord through the spirit of the living God, by faith in Jesus's name.

In the name of the Father, the Son, and the Holy Ghost, be manifested in my brother's character this day, the financial favor of the Lord through the spirit of the living God, by faith in Jesus's name.

In the name of the Father, the Son, and the Holy Ghost, be manifested in my brother's character this day, the miracle waking power of the Lord through the spirit of the living God, by faith in Jesus's name.

In the name of the Father, the Son, and the Holy Ghost, be manifested in my brother's character this day, the understanding of the Lord through the spirit of the living God, by faith in Jesus's name.

In the name of the Father, the Son, and the Holy Ghost,
be manifested in my brother's character this day, the
faith of the Lord through the spirit of the living God, by
faith in Jesus's name.

In the name of the Father, the Son, and the Holy Ghost,
be manifested in my brother's character this day, the
long-suffering of the Lord through the spirit of the living
God, by faith in Jesus's name.

In the name of the Father, the Son, and the Holy Ghost,
be manifested in my brother's character this day, the
gentleness of the Lord through the spirit of the living
God, by faith in Jesus's name.

In the name of the Father, the Son, and the Holy Ghost,
be manifested in my brother's character this day, the
healing gift of the Lord through the spirit of the living
God, by faith in Jesus's name.

In the name of the Father, the Son, and the Holy Ghost,
be manifested in my brother's character this day, the love
of the Lord through the spirit of the living God, by faith
in Jesus's name.

In the name of the Father, the Son, and the Holy Ghost, be manifested in my brother's character this day, the divine protection of the Lord through the spirit of the living God, by faith in Jesus's name.

In the name of the Father, the Son, and the Holy Ghost, be manifested in my brother's character this day, the pastoral grace of the Lord through the spirit of the living God, by faith in Jesus's name.

In the name of the Father, the Son, and the Holy Ghost, be manifested in my brother's character this day, the keys to open the doors of the Lord through the spirit of the living God, by faith in Jesus's name.

In the name of the Father, the Son, and the Holy Ghost, be manifested in my brother's character this day, the apostolic anointing of the Lord through the spirit of the living God, by faith in Jesus's name.

In the name of the Father, the Son, and the Holy Ghost, be manifested in my brother's character this day, the fountain of the Lord through the spirit of the living God, by faith in Jesus's name.

In the name of the Father, the Son, and the Holy Ghost,
be manifested in my brother's character this day, the
evangelistic gift of the Lord through the spirit of the
living God, by faith in Jesus's name.

In the name of the Father, the Son, and the Holy Ghost,
be manifested in my brother's character this day, the
might of the Lord through the spirit of the living God,
by faith in Jesus's name.

In the name of the Father, the Son, and the Holy Ghost,
be manifested in my brother's character this day, the
indwelling of the glory of the Lord through the spirit of
the living God, by faith in Jesus's name.

Chapter Ten

Speaking the Word of God Over My Sisters

In the name of the Father, the Son, and the Holy Ghost, be lifted up in my sister's voice this day; she is the redeem of the Lord through the spirit of the living God, by faith in Jesus's name.

In the name of the Father, the Son, and the Holy Ghost, be lifted up in my sister's voice this day; she is the righteousness of the Lord through the spirit of the living God, by faith in Jesus's name.

In the name of the Father, the Son, and the Holy Ghost, be lifted up in my sister's voice this day; Jesus is the Son of God through the spirit of the living God, by faith in Jesus's name.

In the name of the Father, the Son, and the Holy Ghost, be lifted up in my sister's voice this day; Jesus Christ is the same yesterday, today, and forever through the spirit of the living God, by faith in Jesus's name.

In the name of the Father, the Son, and the Holy Ghost,
be lifted up in my sister's voice this day; all things work
together for good to them that love the Lord through
the spirit of the living God, by faith in Jesus's name.

In the name of the Father, the Son, and the Holy Ghost,
be lifted up in my sister's voice this day; God is good all
the time through the spirit of the living God, by faith in
Jesus's name.

In the name of the Father, the Son, and the Holy Ghost,
be lifted up in my sister's voice this day, righteousness is
exalted, and sin is reproached through the spirit of the
living God, by faith in Jesus's name.

In the name of the Father, the Son, and the Holy Ghost,
be lifted up in my sister's voice this day; Jesus is not
dead. He is still alive through the spirit of the living God,
by faith in Jesus's name.

In the name of the Father, the Son, and the Holy Ghost,
be lifted up in my sister's voice this day; Jesus Christ is a
miracle waking God through the spirit of the living God,
by faith in Jesus's name.

In the name of the Father, the Son, and the Holy Ghost,
be lifted up in my sister's voice this day; Jesus Christ is
seated at the right hand of God the Father through the
spirit of the living God, by faith in Jesus's name.

In the name of the Father, the Son, and the Holy Ghost,
be lifted up in my sister's voice this day; Jesus Christ is
the savior of the world through the spirit of the living
God, by faith in Jesus's name.

In the name of the Father, the Son, and the Holy Ghost,
be lifted up in my sister's voice this day; holiness is
God's standard of living through the spirit of the living
God, by faith in Jesus's name.

In the name of the Father, the Son, and the Holy Ghost,
be lifted up in my sister's voice this day; there is power in
the name of Jesus through the spirit of the living God,
by faith in Jesus's name.

In the name of the Father, the Son, and the Holy Ghost,
be lifted up in my sister's voice this day; absent from her
body, present with the Lord through the spirit of the
living God, by faith in Jesus's name.

In the name of the Father, the Son, and the Holy Ghost,
be lifted up in my sister's voice this day; Jesus Christ is
the word of knowledge through the spirit of the living
God, by faith in Jesus's name.

In the name of the Father, the Son, and the Holy Ghost,
be lifted up in my sister's voice this day; God raised
Jesus Christ from the dead through the spirit of the
living God, by faith in Jesus's name.

In the name of the Father, the Son, and the Holy Ghost,
be lifted up in my sister's voice this day; Jesus Christ is
not a man that he should lie through the spirit of the
living God, by faith in Jesus's name.

In the name of the Father, the Son, and the Holy Ghost,
be lifted up in my sister's voice this day; Jesus Christ is a
lion from the tribe of Judah through the spirit of the
living God, by faith in Jesus's name.

In the name of the Father, the Son, and the Holy Ghost,
be lifted up in my sister's voice this day; Jesus Christ is
the glory of God through the spirit of the living God, by
faith in Jesus's name.

In the name of the Father, the Son, and the Holy Ghost, be lifted up in my sister's voice this day; no one can come to the Father except through Jesus Christ through the spirit of the living God, by faith in Jesus's name.

In the name of the Father, the Son, and the Holy Ghost, be lifted up in my sister's voice this day that Jesus Christ is her soon-coming king through the spirit of the living God, by faith in Jesus's name.

In the name of the Father, the Son, and the Holy Ghost, be lifted up in my sister's voice this day; Jesus Christ is the prince of peace through the spirit of the living God, by faith in Jesus's name.

In the name of the Father, the Son, and the Holy Ghost, be lifted up in my sister's voice this day; Jesus Christ was conceived by the power of the Holy Ghost through the spirit of the living God, by faith in Jesus's name.

In the name of the Father, the Son, and the Holy Ghost, be lifted up in my sister's voice this day; Jesus Christ is the first and last through the spirit of the living God, by faith in Jesus's name.

In the name of the Father, the Son, and the Holy Ghost, be lifted up in my sister's voice this day; Jesus Christ died to save her soul through the spirit of the living God, by faith in Jesus's name.

In the name of the Father, the Son, and the Holy Ghost, be lifted up in my sister's voice this day, Jesus Christ, the Word that became flesh through the spirit of the living God, by faith in Jesus's name.

In the name of the Father, the Son, and the Holy Ghost, be lifted up in my sister's voice this day; Jesus Christ is the Alpha and the Omega through the spirit of the living God, by faith in Jesus's name.

Chapter Eleven

Speaking the Word of God Over Yourself

In the name of the Father, the Son, and the Holy Ghost, be visible in my walk this day and every day of my life; I am the redeemed of the Lord through the spirit of the living God, by faith in Jesus's name.

In the name of the Father, the Son, and the Holy Ghost, be visible in my walk this day and every day of my life; I am the salvation of the Lord through the spirit of the living God, by faith in Jesus's name.

In the name of the Father, the Son, and the Holy Ghost, be visible in my walk this day and every day of my life; I am the righteousness of the Lord through the spirit of the living God, by faith in Jesus's name.

In the name of the Father, the Son, and the Holy Ghost, be visible in my walk this day and every day of my life; I am the righteousness of the Lord through the spirit of the living God, by faith in Jesus's name.

In the name of the Father, the Son, and the Holy Ghost, be visible in my walk this day and every day of my life; I am the blessed of the Lord through the spirit of the living God, by faith in Jesus's name.

In the name of the Father, the Son, and the Holy Ghost, be visible in my walk this day and every day of my life; I am the wisdom of the Lord through the spirit of the living God, by faith in Jesus's name.

In the name of the Father, the Son, and the Holy Ghost, be visible in my walk this day and every day of my life; I am the glory of the Lord through the spirit of the living God, by faith in Jesus's name.

In the name of the Father, the Son, and the Holy Ghost, be visible in my walk this day and every day of my life; I am the holiness of the Lord through the spirit of the living God, by faith in Jesus's name.

In the name of the Father, the Son, and the Holy Ghost, be visible in my walk this day and every day of my life; I am the grace of the Lord through the spirit of the living God, by faith in Jesus's name.

In the name of the Father, the Son, and the Holy Ghost, be visible in my walk this day and every day of my life; I am the peace of the Lord through the spirit of the living God, by faith in Jesus's name.

In the name of the Father, the Son, and the Holy Ghost, be visible in my walk this day and every day of my life; I am the understanding of the Lord through the spirit of the living God, by faith in Jesus's name.

In the name of the Father, the Son, and the Holy Ghost, be visible in my walk this day and every day of my life; I am the fire baptized of the Lord through the spirit of the living God, by faith in Jesus's name.

In the name of the Father, the Son, and the Holy Ghost, be visible in my walk this day and every day of my life; I am the victory of the Lord through the spirit of the living God, by faith in Jesus's name.

In the name of the Father, the Son, and the Holy Ghost, be visible in my walk this day and every day of my life; I am the sole winner of the Lord through the spirit of the living God, by faith in Jesus's name.

In the name of the Father, the Son, and the Holy Ghost,
be visible in my walk this day and every day of my life; I
am the prophet of the Lord through the spirit of the
living God, by faith in Jesus's name.

In the name of the Father, the Son, and the Holy Ghost,
be visible in my walk this day and every day of my life; I
am the miracle worker of the Lord through the spirit of
the living God, by faith in Jesus's name.

In the name of the Father, the Son, and the Holy Ghost,
be visible in my walk this day and every day of my life; I
have the power to get the wealth of the Lord through
the spirit of the living God, by faith in Jesus's name.

In the name of the Father, the Son, and the Holy Ghost,
be visible in my walk this day and every day of my life; I
am an open door of favor of the Lord through the spirit
of the living God, by faith in Jesus's name.

In the name of the Father, the Son, and the Holy Ghost,
be visible in my walk this day and every day of my life; I
am the breadwinner of the Lord through the spirit of the
living God, by faith in Jesus's name.

In the name of the Father, the Son, and the Holy Ghost, be visible in my walk this day and every day of my life; I am the justification of the Lord through the spirit of the living God, by faith in Jesus's name.

In the name of the Father, the Son, and the Holy Ghost, be visible in my walk this day and every day of my life; I am the forgiveness of the Lord through the spirit of the living God, by faith in Jesus's name.

In the name of the Father, the Son, and the Holy Ghost, be visible in my walk this day and every day of my life; I am the might of the Lord through the spirit of the living God, by faith in Jesus's name.

In the name of the Father, the Son, and the Holy Ghost, be visible in my walk this day and every day of my life; I am the meekness of the Lord through the spirit of the living God, by faith in Jesus's name.

In the name of the Father, the Son, and the Holy Ghost, be visible in my walk this day and every day of my life; I am the passion of the Lord through the spirit of the living God, by faith in Jesus's name.

In the name of the Father, the Son, and the Holy Ghost,
be visible in my walk this day and every day of my life; I
am the joy of the Lord through the spirit of the living
God, by faith in Jesus's name.

In the name of the Father, the Son, and the Holy Ghost,
be visible in my walk this day and every day of my life; I
am the gentleness of the Lord through the spirit of the
living God, by faith in Jesus's name.

In the name of the Father, the Son, and the Holy Ghost,
be visible in my walk this day and every day of my life; I
am the compassion of the Lord through the spirit of the
living God, by faith in Jesus's name.

In the name of the Father, the Son, and the Holy Ghost,
be visible in my walk this day and every day of my life; I
am the charity of the Lord through the spirit of the living
God, by faith in Jesus's name.

Chapter Twelve

Faith, Prayer, and Meditation

I pray that this book, through the grace of God that was given to me to write by faith in Jesus Christ, will continue to be a tremendous blessing to you and all the lives that you would have the privilege of the grace of God to speak petition, prophesied, praying over and over the blessings and the favor of God through faith, prayer, and meditation Of God's word.

Meditation is powerful, especially the meditation of God's word. Hebrews 4:12 declares that the meditation of the word can be likened to speaking quickly, powerfully, and sharper than any two-edged sword. The word of God went, spoken, would pierce, dividing asunder of soul and spirit, joints and marrow, also a discerner of the thoughts and the intents of the heart. Therefore, the sharpness of God's word, when spoken by faith in Jesus' name, will definitely cut, heal, and deliver souls, transforming lives for the glory of God.

Meditation is not just repetitiously speaking the words of God over our lives. Consistently day and night to be transformed to the image of God's grace, but every individual we come in contact with day by day, likewise transforming their lives by the written words when spoken over their lives. Therefore, meditation is likened to speaking life, day and night: life over our families, over our parents, over our brothers, over our sisters, over our neighbors, and over our enemies.

Proverbs 18:21. God has given us the power, by way of our tongues, to speak His word by faith to bring restoration and transformation to those that are around us as we live day by day. Meditation is also that of a persistent widow in Luke, chapter 18, who would not take no for an answer but, by her continual coming, asking, calling, and pleading, got her request.

Now listen to what Jesus said in response to the widow's persistent plea to the unjust judge. Verse five says, "Yes, because this widow troubled me, I will avenge her lest by her continual coming, she weary me." Versus 6-8, Jesus further said,

"Hear what the unjust judge said and shall not God avenge his own elect which cry day and night unto Him, though he bear long with them. I tell you that he will avenge them speedily. Nevertheless, when the Son of man cometh, Shall He find faith on the earth? Meditation of God's word consumes spirit, soul, and body. The agent of God's transforming grace through the spirit of the living God, by faith in Jesus' name, reconciling man back to God.

The question may be asked, what is the meditation of God's word? First, it may or can be said that it is the constant spoken word of God that comes out of our mouths day and night. Second, it is the repetitious, pondering in our hearts, the word of God that is acceptable in his sight as Lord and Redeemer. Psalms 19:14.

Meditation, as I reiterate, is an influential power in changing the direction of our future and destiny. If a man is unable to control or modify his meditation, he will not be able to chart the course directing his life into a better future. Therefore, one must be able to cast down one's imagination.

Second Corinthians 10:5 bringing his or her thoughts under the obedience of Christ. Meditation is strongly expressed to the servant of God, the Apostle Paul in Philippians 4:13, that he can do all things by the will of God through faith in Jesus Christ. We must understand that our sufficiency or being adequate is none of ourselves. Therefore, our sufficiency to become the creature that God designed us to be is by having faith in one name, in the heavens above, and one name in and under the earth beneath, that is, the name of Jesus Christ. Philippians 2:10-11.

The word of God declares in Jeshua 1:8, one concerning meditation. God commanded the children of Israel to meditate on the book of the law, day and night, not allowing the word of God to depart or leave their mouth, but continue to ponder, speaking over and over day and night, the law. As a result, the book of the law shall make them wise, prosperous, and having good success.

Meditation, Psalms 1 verses 2-3, day and night, cause an individual to become like a tree planted by the rivers of water. Day and night meditation on God's words guarantees that your leaves shall not wither. In other words, whatsoever you do shall prosper in the name of

Father, in the name of the Son, and in the name of the Holy Ghost, by faith in Jesus' name.

Also, the wisdom of God's meditated word, day and night, a floating river of living waters of the heart, revealing the understanding and the fear of the Lord. Proverbs 1:7. Yes, the fear of the Lord is the beginning of knowledge. Likewise, the fear or reverence of God is to depart from evils. Proverbs 3:7.

Meditation, therefore, as a man thinketh in his heart God's word, the mouth speaketh it. The wisdom of God, the word that is seasoned with grace. Colossians 4:6, KJV, "Let your speech be always with grace, seasoned with salt that ye may know how ye ought to answer every man, by faith in Jesus' name.

Meditation is looking back to ponder the tender mercies of God. Reminiscing the goodness of the Lord and how he brought you this far by faith through many dangerous toils and snares, such amazing grace.

Meditation is, I will remember, the years of the right hand of the Most High. Meditation is, I will remember the many years of blessings and favor being recalled in my heart as the mercies of God are revealed in my heart day and night. Psalms 77:8-9.

Meditation is Psalms 77-11; remember the works of the Lord. The psalmist declares that He will remember the wonderous works of old, the miraculous signs and wonders that will continually baffle the minds of unbelievers. The psalmist reiterated in verse 11 that he would meditate on all the works of God, talking and testifying of His doings.

The wisdom gained through meditating on God's Word brings understanding and the fear of the Lord, the beginning of true knowledge. It enables us to depart from evil and walk in righteousness. Therefore, let our speech always be seasoned with grace, reflecting the wisdom of God in our interactions with others.

In the name of the Father, the Son, and the Holy Spirit, may glory be given through the reading, meditation, and constant speaking of the words contained within this book. May it inspire and transform not only our families and communities but also our own lives. May it draw us closer to God, deepening our faith and ushering us into a future filled with divine purpose and abundant blessings. Amen.

Meditation is the constant utterance of God's Word, both spoken and pondered within our hearts. It is the acceptance of His Word as our guide, aligning our thoughts and imaginations with the obedience of Christ. Through faith in Jesus, we find sufficiency, and by His name, we become all that God intended us to be.

I pray that as you close this chapter and reflect upon the words written here, your spirit is ignited with a renewed sense of purpose and an unwavering faith in Jesus Christ. May the grace of God continue to flow through every word and page of this book, bringing forth blessings and favor in your life and the lives of those you touch.

Thanks, honor, and glory to Almighty God for all those He has allowed to support this book and will continue to support. The favor and the wisdom to write by the grace of God. Thank God for the Divine Ghost writer's family. Thank God for the body of Christ's family. Also, thank God for my biological family, and therefore, once again, thank God for your prayers, your coaching, your financial, or any other spiritual or temporal support. To God be all the glory, to God be all the glory, through the spirit of the living God by faith in Jesus' name, Amen.

www.ingramcontent.com/pod-product-compliance
Lightning Source LLC
Chambersburg PA
CBHW050546160726
48003CB00002B/775